DINOSAUR DISCOVERY

EVERYTHING YOU NEED TO BE A PALEONTOLOGIST

CHRIS McGOWAN

Illustrated by ERICA LYN SCHMIDT

SIMON & SCHUSTER BOOKS FOR YOUNG READERS
NEW YORK   LONDON   TORONTO   SYDNEY

NOTE: This book includes suggestions for activities
that will help the reader understand the many unique features and abilities
of dinosaurs. The activities are intended for children to do with the help and supervision
of a parent or other adult. Most of these activities can be done with items found
around the house or that are otherwise readily available.

So, young readers and dinosaur discoverers: Please make sure to involve a parent
or other adult as you set up and do the activities, and have a great time!

SIMON & SCHUSTER BOOKS FOR YOUNG READERS

An imprint of Simon & Schuster Children's Publishing Division

1230 Avenue of the Americas, New York, New York 10020

Text copyright © 2011 by Chris McGowan

Illustrations copyright © 2011 by Erica Lyn Schmidt

SIMON & SCHUSTER BOOKS FOR YOUNG READERS is a trademark of Simon & Schuster, Inc.

For information about special discounts for bulk purchases,

please contact Simon & Schuster Special Sales at 1-866-506-1949 or business@simonandschuster.com.

The Simon & Schuster Speakers Bureau can bring authors to your live event.

For more information or to book an event, contact the Simon & Schuster Speakers Bureau

at 1-866-248-3049 or visit our website at www.simonspeakers.com.

Book design by Laurent Linn and Tom Daly

The text for this book is set in Alinea Roman.

The illustrations for this book are rendered in watercolor paints.

Manufactured in China

0411 SCP

2 4 6 8 10 9 7 5 3 1

Library of Congress Cataloging-in-Publication Data

McGowan, Christopher.

Dinosaur discovery : everything you need to be a paleontologist / Chris McGowan ;

illustrated by Erica Lyn Schmidt. — 1st ed.

p. cm.

ISBN 978-1-4169-4764-6 (hardcover)

1. Paleontology—Juvenile literature. 2. Paleontologists—Vocational guidance—Juvenile literature.

I. Schmidt, Erica Lyn, ill. II. Title.

QE714.5.M34 2010

560—dc22

2009044604

PHOTO/ILLUSTRATION CREDITS

Photograph of Othniel Marsh (p. 6) from the Library of Congress, Prints & Photographs Division, LC-DIG-cwpbh-04124 • Photograph of ichthyosaur specimen (p. 25, top right) printed with thanks to the Staatliches Museum für Naturkunde Stuttgart <http://www.naturkundemuseum-bw.de/stuttgart/> • Illustration of dinner party (p. 28) reprinted from the *London Illustrated News*, January 7, 1854, Vol. 24, no. 662, p. 22 • Images of Gideon Mantell (p. 29) and Mary Anning (p. 34) reprinted with permission from the Natural History Museum, London • Photograph of *Triceratops* bone (p. 44) reprinted with permission from Kenneth H. Olson, and with thanks to Greg Erickson • Photograph of tooth replica (p. 44) copyright © 1996 by the Society of Vertebrate Paleontology. Reprinted with permission of the SVP. • Photograph of *Tyrannosaurus* tooth (p. 44) printed with thanks to the Royal Saskatchewan Museum, and to Karen Chin • Photograph of bone under microscope (p. 45) from Mary H. Schweitzer et al. "Soft-tissue vessels and cellular preservation in *Tyrannosaurus rex.*" *Science*, 2005, Vol. 307, pp. 1952–1955. Reprinted with permission from AAAS.

*To John Attridge, without whose mentorship I would
never have become a paleontologist*
—C. M.

*To my best friend and husband, Tony, thank you for the unconditional
love and sacrifice you've shown to make this possible. You'll always be my
favorite. To my parents, thank you for being crazy enough to let me attend
art school in the first place! To my family and friends, the encouragement
you gave me meant more than you realize. And to Sam,
thank you for finding our ruby slippers.*
—E. L. S.

Acknowledgments

This book has had a long gestation period, and a large number of people have helped me over the years—from paleontological colleagues, who have supplied me with illustrations and information on their research, to my grandchildren, who have participated in the experiments. I am deeply grateful to you all.

Jill Grinberg, my literary agent, facilitated this project from the outset, making an idea into a reality. I am indeed fortunate to have such a driving force.

My sincere thanks to Justin Chanda, of Simon & Schuster, for his enthusiasm and support of the initial project. I also thank my editor, Alexandra Cooper, for her help and for her indefatigable endurance. Thanks also to Ariel Colletti for her editorial assistance. I also wish to thank Cheryl Pientka, of Jill Grinberg Literary Management, for her continued support and encouragement.

Erica Lyn Schmidt is an artist of considerable talent, as anyone familiar with her sentient images knows. I thank her for her innate understanding of her subjects, and for being able to produce so many illustrations in such a constrained time frame. Working with her has been a great privilege and pleasure.
—C. M.

ALLOSAURUS

(pronounced AL-oh-SOR-us)

MEANING OF NAME: "Different reptile"
TYPE: Theropod
AGE: Late Jurassic
LOCALITY: Western North America and Portugal
LENGTH: 40 feet (12 m)

CARNIVOROUS DINOSAURS ARE MORE UNCOMMON THAN **HERBIVOROUS** ONES, but there are many skeletons of Allosaurus. Like other carnivorous dinosaurs, Allosaurus was **bipedal**, walking on two legs. Weighing about 2 tons, it was one quarter as heavy as Tyrannosaurus. The 3-foot-long (1 m) skull is deep from top to bottom, but narrow from side to side. Its large openings and narrow bones make it look flimsy. However, a computer study using 3-D X-ray pictures shows it was remarkably strong. The bite, though, was probably weak—unlike Tyrannosaurus, whose forceful jaws could smash through bones. Using its strong neck, Allosaurus may have slashed at its prey with jaws wide open, tearing out great chunks of flesh with its daggerlike teeth.

PELVIS The three-pronged **Saurischian** ("lizard-hipped") pelvis was attached to the vertebral column (backbone) by the upper bone, called the ilium. Many of the leg muscles attached to the pelvis.

pubis

ilium

ischium

POSTURE Allosaurus probably held its backbone horizontally. The tail would have been used to balance the weight of the rest of the body.

— DID YOU KNOW? —

DINOSAUR GRAVEYARD Thousands of Allosaurus bones—all jumbled up—have been collected from the Cleveland-Lloyd Dinosaur Quarry in Utah. This may have been a swamp that trapped dinosaurs.

TEETH The teeth are serrated, like steak knives, to cut through flesh. They are set in deep sockets, which prevented them from being ripped out.

serrations

WISHBONE A wishbone (furcula)—found in all flying birds—was recently discovered in *Allosaurus*. This reinforces the idea that birds are closely related to dinosaurs.

APATOSAURUS

(pronounced ah-PAT-oh-SOR-us)

MEANING OF NAME: "Illusionary reptile"
TYPE: Sauropod
AGE: Late Jurassic
LOCALITY: Western North America
LENGTH: 70 feet (21 m)

APATOSAURUS, WITH ITS LONG NECK AND TAIL, SMALL HEAD, AND HUGE BODY, is what many people picture when they hear the word "dinosaur." A member of the **sauropods**, *Apatosaurus*—once called *Brontosaurus*—was the first one assembled, or **mounted**, for public display. The name *Apatosaurus* was chosen because some of the tail-bones were like those of a giant extinct lizard.

Weighing almost 30 tons, *Apatosaurus* had a skeleton made to withstand huge forces. The legs are heavily built—like the pelvis and shoulders—and the bones were kept straight in line. Similarly, elephants stand and walk straight-legged to reduce the forces on their bones. Aside from being thick, sauropod leg bones are solid, giving additional strength. Most other land animals, from mice to horses to humans, have hollow limb bones.

TWO NAMES In 1877 Othniel Charles Marsh named *Apatosaurus* based on a few bones. Two years later he named *Brontosaurus* ("thunder lizard") based on an almost complete skeleton. Later studies showed they were the same kind of dinosaur.

STOMACH STONES *Apatosaurus*, like many dinosaurs, including other sauropods, swallowed stones. This helped it grind up its food. Modern birds do the same thing.

FORKED VERTEBRAE The neural spines in the neck and shoulder regions are forked. This probably formed a groove for a thick **nuchal** (neck) **ligament**, which supported the head and neck.

TEETH The teeth are slender, like pencils. Found only in the front of the mouth, they were used for gathering plants, not for chewing.

FAKING ROCK

Fossils are found in layered rocks, which usually formed in seas, lakes, and rivers when sediment in the water settled onto the bottom. Over thousands of years these layers became squashed together, forming **sedimentary rock**. You can fake some yourself.

1. You'll need: a glass screw-top jar about the size of a soda can; sand; soil from your backyard or garden center (*not* potting soil); a tablespoon; water; clear adhesive (UHU suggested); a Styrofoam or paper cup; a plate; a pencil; scissors.

2. Pour 1 tablespoon (15 ml) of sand and the same amount of soil into the jar. Add 6 tablespoons of water. Screw on the lid and shake the jar hard. Allow the sediment to settle for 30 minutes. Layers form, with sand at the bottom.

3. Shake the jar again. Add 2 tablespoons of glue, and shake the jar some more. Quickly pour the mixture into the cup, scraping all the sludge from the jar. The foam that forms at the top soon disappears—gently blowing on it helps. Leave the cup overnight.

4. Carefully move the cup over to the plate. Using a pencil, stab a hole through the side of the cup about halfway down to drain some liquid. Repeat with progressively lower holes until you see the surface of the sediment. Make your last hole at the surface. Tilt *slightly* to drain off the water. Leave to dry for two days.

5. Put the cup into a freezer for 1 hour. Using scissors, cut off the top of the cup down to the level of the sediment. Carefully tear away the rest of the cup. Leave it to dry on the plate for one day before handling. The main difference between fake and real rock is that the sediment is cemented together with glue, rather than through the action of tons of pressure over millions of years.

STANDING UP TO FORCE

Skeletons—like buildings, airplanes, and other structures—are built to take the forces pushing and pulling against them, without breaking. A table, for example, usually has vertical legs. You could safely sit on such a table because its legs are positioned to support large forces. However, if its legs were slanting out sideways, it might collapse under your weight. The bones in the skull of *Allosaurus* are similarly lined up, to withstand the force of biting into prey. You can see the importance of this with a simple experiment.

1. You'll need: two toilet paper tubes; a pile of books.

2. Stand one of the tubes vertically. Carefully place a book on top so that the center of its cover lines up with the center of the tube. Add books, one at a time. As the pile grows, you may need a helper to keep it steady.

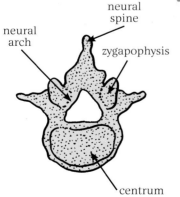

3. Continue until the tube collapses. Are you surprised at how many books it supported?

4. Lay the second tube horizontally. Place a book on top of the tube, centering it like a level teeter-totter—keep holding the book in place. Using your other hand, continue adding books as before. You'll see the tube is much weaker in this position.

CHECKING YOUR VERTEBRAL COLUMN

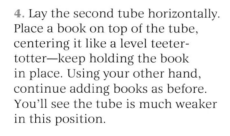

neural spine
neural arch
zygapophysis
centrum

The individual bones of your vertebral column, called vertebrae, have the same basic pattern. Each vertebra has a main part, the centrum, shaped like a doughnut. Above this is the neural arch, through which the spinal cord runs. Above the neural arch is the neural spine. You can feel the tips of your neural spines by bending your head forward and running your fingers down your neck. Designed for different roles, the vertebrae vary from neck to trunk to tail. (You *do* have a tail, but it's too short to show.)

Your vertebrae, like the other bones in your body, are joined together by tough, flexible cords called **ligaments**. Animals with backbones are called **vertebrates**.

All you need for this activity is a long mirror. While standing in front of the mirror, keep your body straight and try touching your shoulder with your head. Now try bending your body to the side. You'll find your neck is far more flexible than your trunk—it's designed that way.

BARE BONES

When you have chicken for dinner, save the bones. You can use the **femur** (thighbone), tibia (shinbone), or humerus (upper arm bone). Pop them in a plastic bag and ask permission to keep them in the freezer. When you've got a good haul, you can start cleaning them.

1. You'll need: chicken bones; a plastic bag; an old toothbrush or scouring pad.

2. Ask an adult helper to boil the bones for about 30 minutes. Afterward rinse them in cold water and remove the meat and gristle by scrubbing them with the old toothbrush or plastic scouring pad.

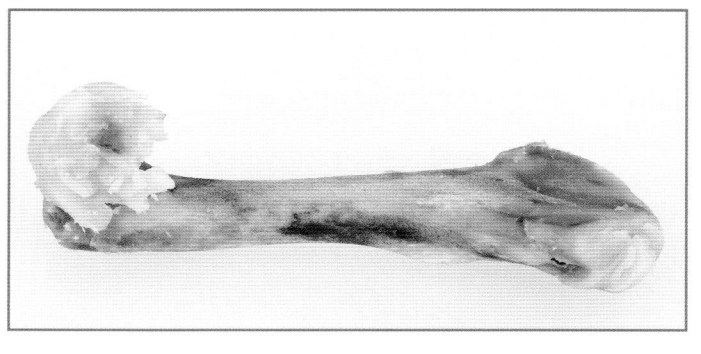

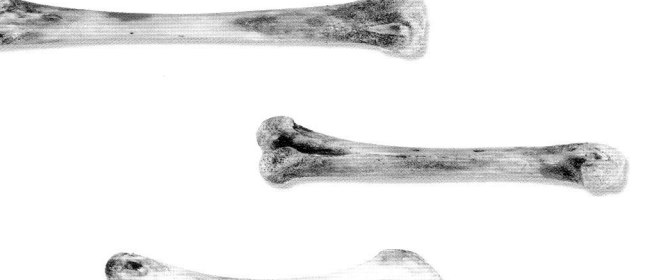

3. Notice the thick white caps of cartilage at either end of the bones. These show that the chickens were young and still growing. In adults the cartilage, which forms smooth surfaces for the joints, is quite thin. Don't worry if the cartilages come off; you don't need them. Leave the bones to dry overnight. (If you have a cat or dog, make sure to keep the bones out of its reach—it'll crunch them otherwise.) You'll be using the dried bones in the next activity.

BREAKING BONES

Bone has two main parts: a calcium-rich mineral called **apatite**, which makes it hard and stiff, and a protein called **collagen**, which makes it tough and elastic. You can test this for yourself.

1. You'll need: three similar dried chicken bones (the tibia is probably best); some vinegar; a small Ziploc bag.

2. Leave the first bone in vinegar in the Ziploc bag for ten days—this dissolves the apatite. Ask an adult to put the second bone into the oven at 300°F (150°C) for 2 hours—this breaks down the collagen. Leave the third bone untreated.

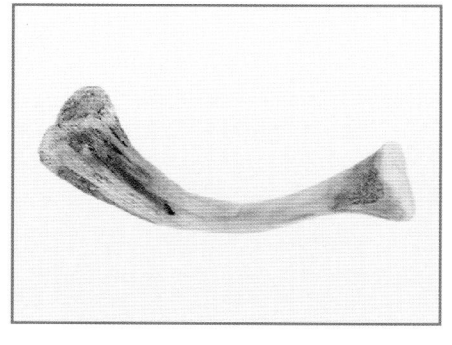

The first bone, now mostly collagen, feels soft and rubbery and can be bent.

The second bone is still hard and stiff, but it's brittle and no longer tough. Try breaking it—it'll snap like a cookie.

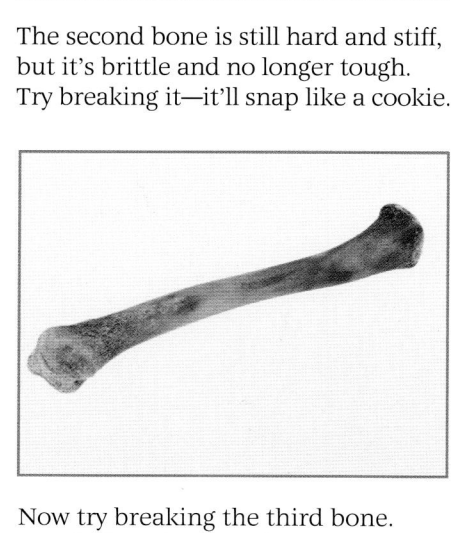

Now try breaking the third bone. Tough, isn't it? If you had to break a fresh *Apatosaurus* bone, you would need some *really* heavy equipment!

FAKING FOSSIL FEATHERS

When *Archaeopteryx* was discovered, people were puzzled that something as delicate as a feather could fossilize. The explanation is simple. During the late Jurassic most of Germany was covered by sea. As sediments settled on the seabed, they became flattened into stone. Because the sediments were very fine, the stone is smooth—so smooth that it was used in printing and is called lithographic ("stone drawing") limestone. Imagine *Archaeopteryx* sinking to the seabed. As more sediments settled on top, it became pressed into the firmer bottom, leaving imprints of its feathers. Thousands of years later, long after the feathers had rotted away, the sediments hardened into rock. You can fake this process.

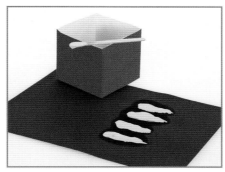

1. You'll need: plaster of paris (from a craft store); a teaspoon; water; an empty container for mixing; a Popsicle stick; a sheet of paper; a feather (look for quills from a craft store). A magnifying glass is useful for examining your results.

2. Mix a heaping teaspoon of powder with a teaspoon of water, stirring well. It should be like toothpaste. Using the Popsicle stick, make several thin smears on the paper—each one at least as wide as your feather—smoothing as you go. Wait 30–45 seconds, then *gently* touch them—they should barely mark your finger. If they leave a wet mark, wait another 15 seconds.

3. Gently press the feather against the plaster smears, stroking it several times to press it down. Remove the feather. (If the feather gets covered in plaster, wash it off and dry it with a tissue. Wait a minute for the plaster to firm up before proceeding.)

4. Repeat for all the smears. You should see feather impressions in the plaster. When they set, you have fake fossils.

FLYING FEATHERS

A bird's wing—like an airplane's—has a curved top surface, like a Frisbee. This creates lift. You can check this with a simple demonstration. Place a sheet of paper on a table as if you were going to write upon it. Move it toward you so that the bottom edge overhangs the table by an inch (2.5 cm) or so. With your thumbs on top, pick the paper up so that the other end droops down. Gently blow across the curved upper surface. Your paper "wing" lifts. Wing feathers are like tiny wings, so you can make them fly.

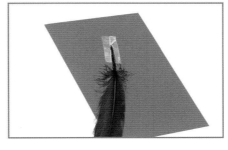

1. You'll need: a wing feather; Scotch tape; a piece of cardboard as long as the feather. Check that your feather is slightly curved along its length and when seen end-on.

2. Attach a *small* strip of tape, about ¼ inch x ³/₁₆ inch (7 mm x 5 mm) long, to the tip of the quill (the pointed end of the feather) so that it lines up with the feather. Cover the sticky side with a second small strip of tape to make a tab.

3. Lay the feather on the card so that it arches away from the surface, like a bridge. Using another small strip of tape, attach the tab to the card—make sure the feather is level, with its two edges the same distance above the surface. The feather should freely hinge up and down. Keeping your lips level with the feather, gently blow. Watch the feather lift off.

11

ARCHAEOPTERYX

(pronounced AR-kee-OP-ter-ix)

MEANING OF NAME:	"Ancient wing"
TYPE:	Bird (also theropod)
AGE:	Late Jurassic
LOCALITY:	Germany
LENGTH:	2 feet (0.6 m)

HANDS *Archaeopteryx* has three separate fingers, like most theropod dinosaurs. Embryonic birds have three fingers too, but this changes before they hatch, and chicks usually have just one separate finger, like adult birds.

THE DISCOVERY OF THE FIRST *ARCHAEOPTERYX* SKELETON caused great excitement in 1861 because feather impressions were stamped into the surrounding rock. This had to be a bird—it had feathers, wings, and a wishbone—but it was as ancient as the dinosaurs. And as later discoveries showed, it had many dinosaur features, including teeth, clawed fingers, and a long, bony tail. If we saw one of these chicken-size animals flying overhead, we'd probably think it was just an unfamiliar bird. However, it has a **theropod** skeleton and is now included in that group, along with modern birds. So technically, birds *are* dinosaurs.

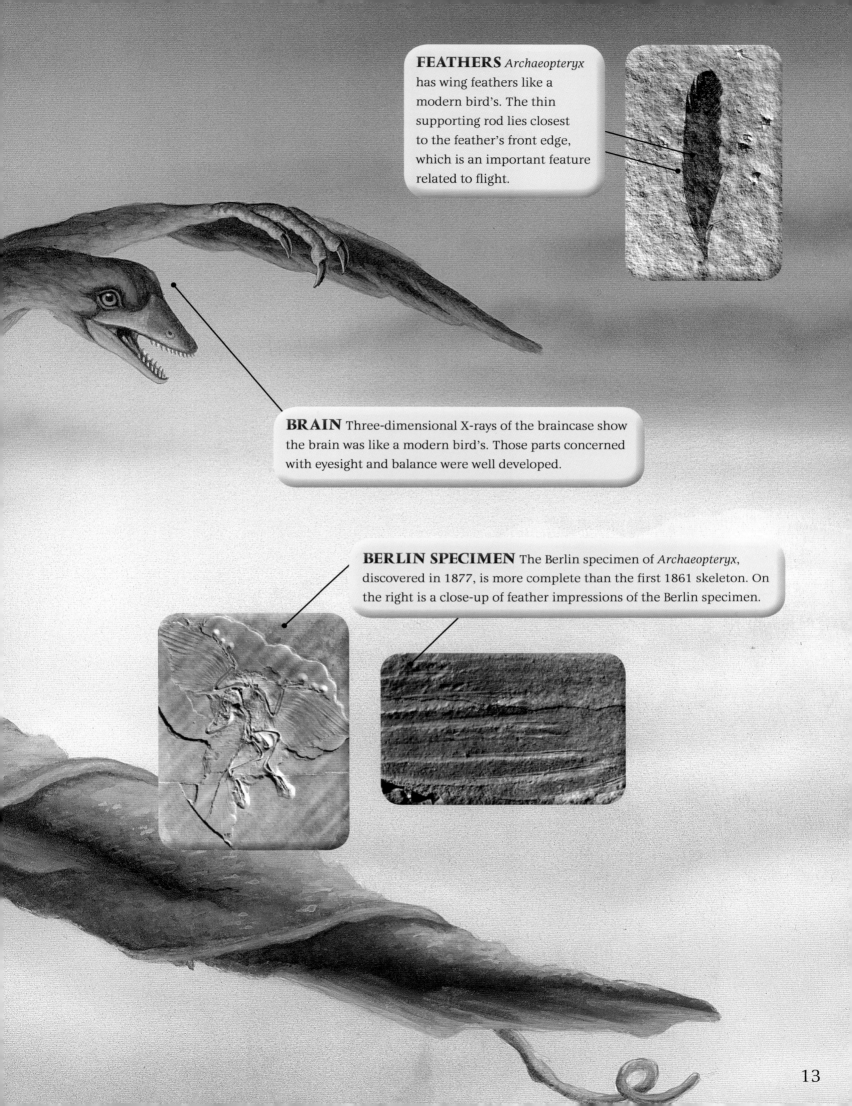

FEATHERS *Archaeopteryx* has wing feathers like a modern bird's. The thin supporting rod lies closest to the feather's front edge, which is an important feature related to flight.

BRAIN Three-dimensional X-rays of the braincase show the brain was like a modern bird's. Those parts concerned with eyesight and balance were well developed.

BERLIN SPECIMEN The Berlin specimen of *Archaeopteryx*, discovered in 1877, is more complete than the first 1861 skeleton. On the right is a close-up of feather impressions of the Berlin specimen.

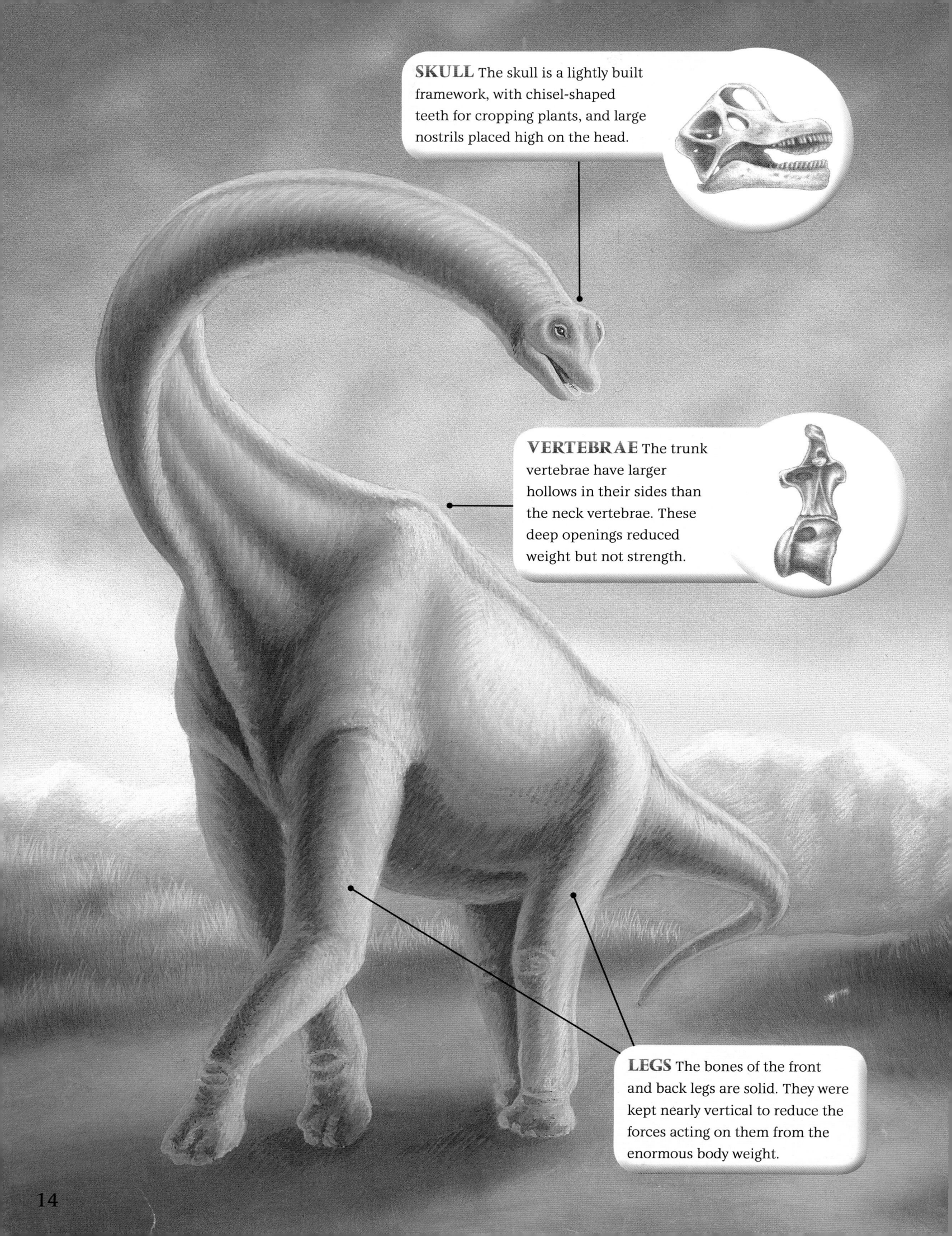

SKULL The skull is a lightly built framework, with chisel-shaped teeth for cropping plants, and large nostrils placed high on the head.

VERTEBRAE The trunk vertebrae have larger hollows in their sides than the neck vertebrae. These deep openings reduced weight but not strength.

LEGS The bones of the front and back legs are solid. They were kept nearly vertical to reduce the forces acting on them from the enormous body weight.

BRACHIOSAURUS

(pronounced BRAK-ee-oh-SOR-us)

MEANING OF NAME:	"Arm reptile"
TYPE:	Sauropod
AGE:	Late Jurassic
LOCALITY:	Mostly North America, and East Africa
LENGTH:	75 feet (23 m)

UNLIKE MOST SAUROPODS, *Brachiosaurus* has front legs that are longer than its back legs, so the vertebral column tilts upward, from hips to shoulders. *Brachiosaurus* was first discovered in Colorado in 1900, but the best finds were made a few years later in Tanzania, East Africa. Field crews from Berlin's Humboldt Museum dug out nearly 250 tons of fossils. Most were sauropods, and the prize was *Brachiosaurus*. Nobody had ever mounted such a huge dinosaur—a horse could walk between its legs—and it's still the biggest mounted dinosaur today. The largest neck vertebrae are 5 feet (1.5 m) long. But if you tried lifting one, you'd be amazed at its lightness. Beautifully built to reduce weight, the vertebrae have thin webs and struts of bone, and large hollows in the sides of the centrum. The leg bones, in contrast, are heavily built.

— DID YOU KNOW? —

LAND OR WATER? Early paleontologists thought *Brachiosaurus* was too heavy to live on land. Having its nostrils on top of the skull, like a whale, suggested it lived in water. We now think all sauropods were land dwellers.

FINDING YOUR CENTER OF MASS

The **center of mass** (or center of gravity) is the balance point of an object. Balance a ruler on your finger and you'll find the center of mass lies at the halfway point. That's because rulers are the same width throughout—bodies are not so simple.

1. You'll need: a board at least as long as your height (a length of two-by-four works); a broom handle; an adult assistant; tape. Do this on an uncarpeted floor.

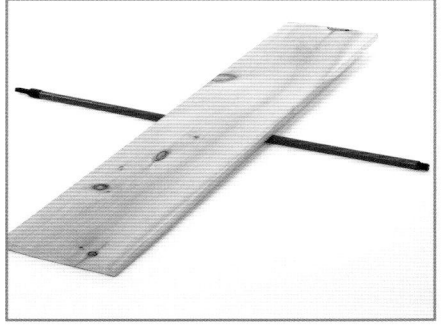

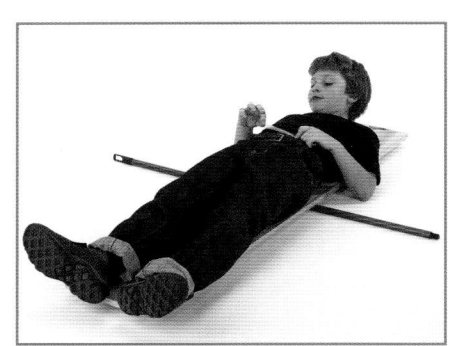

2. Balance the board on the handle like a teeter-totter. Lie down on the board, making sure the top of your head and your heels are the same distance from either end. Press your arms against your sides. Ask your assistant to roll the handle, one way or the other, until the board balances. The handle now lies beneath your center of mass. Get your assistant to mark the level on your body with tape.

3. Your center of mass probably lies about a hand's width below your navel. If you are younger than about nine, it's probably level with your navel.

4. You could mark a dot on your skin at this level, in line with your navel, but this wouldn't be your exact center of mass—that lies beneath your skin, in the middle of your body.

I BEAMS

Imagine building a high-rise apartment. Each new story adds more weight. Vertical columns of concrete support this enormous load. They act like table legs, though there are many more than four. Horizontal steel beams attach to the columns to support each floor. The beam looks like a capital letter I when seen from one end, so it's called an I beam. It is built this way to be strong without being too heavy. If you cut across the end of the centrum of a sauropod's trunk vertebra, you'd see it was like an I beam. A simple experiment shows why I beams are stronger than flat beams.

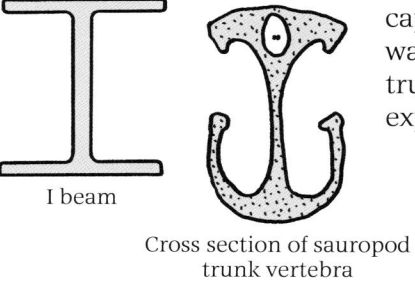

I beam

Cross section of sauropod trunk vertebra

1. You'll need two Popsicle sticks.

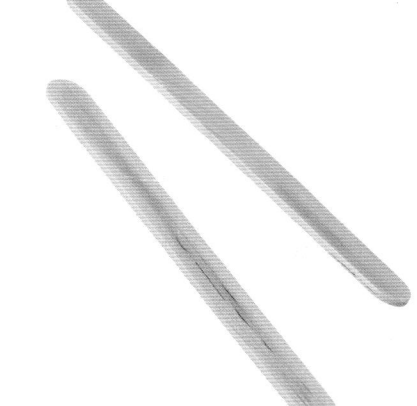

2. Hold one of the sticks flat between your fingers and thumbs. If you try bending it, you'll find it's quite springy. You're bending the stick as if it were a flat beam. Try breaking it. The stick snaps easily.

3. Hold the second stick upright along its edges—this is tricky and you'll have to grip firmly. Can you feel it bending? Not a chance! This is because you're bending the stick as if it were an I beam. Try breaking it—you'll probably fail.

BALANCING ACT

Now that you've found your center of mass, here's another experiment to try.

1. You'll need: a paper clip; a length of string or thread; tape; a bag weighted with books—not too heavy to hold at arm's length.

2. Tie the paper clip to one end of the string. Tape the other end to your body at the level of your center of mass, in line with your navel.

3. Adjust its length so that the paper clip almost touches the floor when you lean forward. With feet apart and in line, hold your hands behind your back and lean forward. The paper clip will hover just in front of your toes, midway between your feet. As long as your center of mass stays between your feet, you won't fall.

4. Lift one foot and you'll immediately topple. Now balance on one foot and see how the paper clip dangles above it. Balancing on one leg requires the center of mass to be in line with the foot on the ground.

6. Now hold the bag out behind you. This shifts your center of mass back a little, allowing you to lean farther forward. Imagine how far you could lean if you had a long tail like *Deinonychus*. Swing the bag forward—you'll immediately lose balance.

5. Stand on both feet again, but this time hold the bag in one hand. Keeping the bag beside your leg, lean forward until you almost topple.

CAT'S CLAWS

For this activity you'll need a friendly cat.

1. Look closely at one of the cat's paws. You probably won't see its claws because they're retracted. All you'll see is the soft pads at the ends of the toes.

2. Push gently against a pad, and the claw will pop out. (If your cat has been declawed, look at the back ones—they're usually intact.) Cats can do this at will by flexing certain muscles—so could *Deinonychus*.

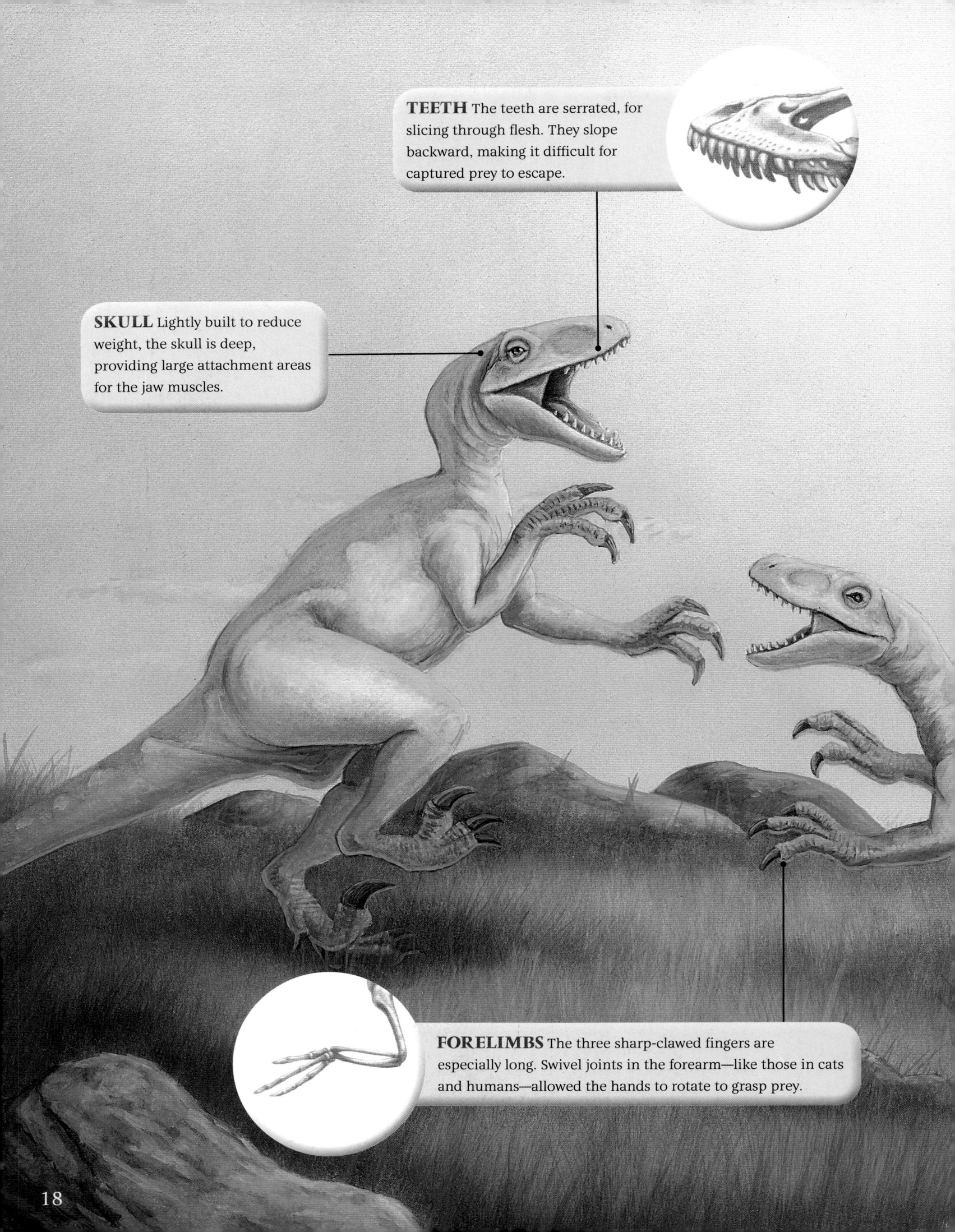

TEETH The teeth are serrated, for slicing through flesh. They slope backward, making it difficult for captured prey to escape.

SKULL Lightly built to reduce weight, the skull is deep, providing large attachment areas for the jaw muscles.

FORELIMBS The three sharp-clawed fingers are especially long. Swivel joints in the forearm—like those in cats and humans—allowed the hands to rotate to grasp prey.

DEINONYCHUS

(pronounced die-NON-i-kus)

MEANING OF NAME: "Terrible claw"
TYPE: Theropod
AGE: Early Cretaceous
LOCALITY: Western North America
LENGTH: 10 feet (3 m)

WHILE DINOSAUR HUNTING IN MONTANA IN 1964, Yale paleontologist John Ostrom discovered a bizarre new carnivore. Like most theropods, *Deinonychus* has three large toes pointing forward, with a small "big toe" pointing back. What amazed Ostrom was that the inside toe ended in a huge curved claw. The wraparound joint surfaces showed it could swing back, clear of the ground. Cats also retract (pull back) their claws to keep them sharp. So *Deinonychus* walked on only two toes. The curved claw had one purpose: slashing and killing. Balancing on one foot while slashing with the other required special modifications in the skeleton. The most remarkable is in the tail. The vertebrae at its base have the usual small **zygapophyses**, but these become so long in the rest of the tail that they overlap the vertebrae in front. This results in a rigid tail, which was used, like a tightrope walker's pole, for balancing.

PELVIS Most of the muscles that retracted the femur—driving the leg back—were attached to the pubis. This was especially long and sloped back, giving the leg a wide swing.

pubis

EUOPLOCEPHALUS

(pronounced YOU-oh-plo-SEF-ah-lus)

MEANING OF NAME:	"Well-armored head"
TYPE:	Ankylosaur
AGE:	Late Cretaceous
LOCALITY:	Western North America
LENGTH:	20 feet (6 m)

NOSTRILS Each nostril led into a looped passageway with side branches, recently reconstructed using 3-D X-rays (visit http://www.youtube.com/watch?v=6Qqf8UotDiU). This complicated system—found in all ankylosaurs—may have improved their sense of smell, helping them to avoid predators.

SKULL The broad, heavy skull had a toothless beak, something like a parrot's, used for cropping plants.

TEETH The teeth, set in single rows in the cheek region, have long roots. But the chisel-shaped crowns are only about ¼ inch (7 mm) high.

20

Built like a battle tank, *Euoplocephalus* was the ultimate defensive dinosaur. The heavy hips were expanded into shields at the back, with similar shoulder shields in front. Most of the armor was provided by curved bone plates embedded in the hide, reinforced with knobs and spikes. As these plates were separate, the body had some flexibility. A solid shield of plates protected the skull—there was even a plate embedded in the eyelid. The long tail ended in a heavy, bony club, used to fend off attackers. As in *Deinonychus*, the tail was rigid except at its base—smashing an attacking dinosaur's shins with a stiff club would have inflicted maximum damage. The short, stocky legs—built for plodding, not running—gave a low-slung posture, like a hippo rather than a horse.

ACTIVITIES

When **quadrupeds** (four-footed animals) walk or run, they have to take one or more feet off the ground. Quadrupeds can stand on three legs as long as their center of mass stays between the feet on the ground. You can test this.

1. You'll need: a paper clip; string or thread; Scotch tape; a piece of elastic (or a string of elastic bands) at least twice as long as your arm. A helper would be useful.

2. Tie the paper clip to one end of the string. Tape the other end to your body at the level of your center of mass, in line with your navel (see "Finding Your Center of Mass," page 16). Adjust the string so that the paper clip just touches your knee.

3. Join the two ends of the elastic together to make a closed loop. With legs apart, stretch the elastic between your feet, stepping down to hold it in place. Hold the other two corners of the rubber rectangle between your thumbs.

Without letting go, squat down to stand like a quadruped. The paper clip should be dangling just above the floor—adjust the string if necessary.

4. Release the elastic from one foot to form a triangle. The paper clip hovers inside the triangle, so when you lift that foot, you won't topple.

Repeat the experiment, but this time release the elastic from one hand. The paper clip should lie outside the triangle. If it doesn't, ask an adult to do the experiment and then it will. Do you expect to topple when you lift your hand? Try it and see.

How hard could an ankylosaur have hit with its club if its tail was flexible rather than stiff? You can get some idea with a simple experiment.

1. You'll need: some modeling clay; two drinking straws.

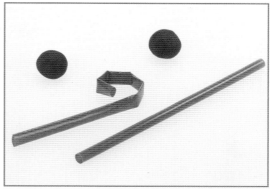

2. Make two balls of modeling clay about ½ to ¾ inch (13 to 20 mm) in diameter—they need to be the same size. Bend over the last ½ inch (13 mm) of one of the straws. Continue folding over the remainder—this will put kinks into the straw, making it more flexible.

3. Attach a ball to the end of each straw, making sure it's firmly attached. Holding the flexible straw so that the kinks are vertical, strike the corner of something solid, like a desk. Strike several more times. The depth of the marks in the modeling clay gives some idea of the force of the blows. Repeat using the rigid straw. Which one hit harder?

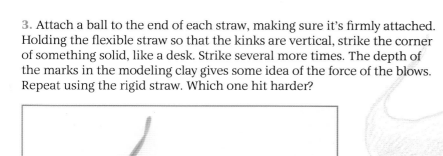

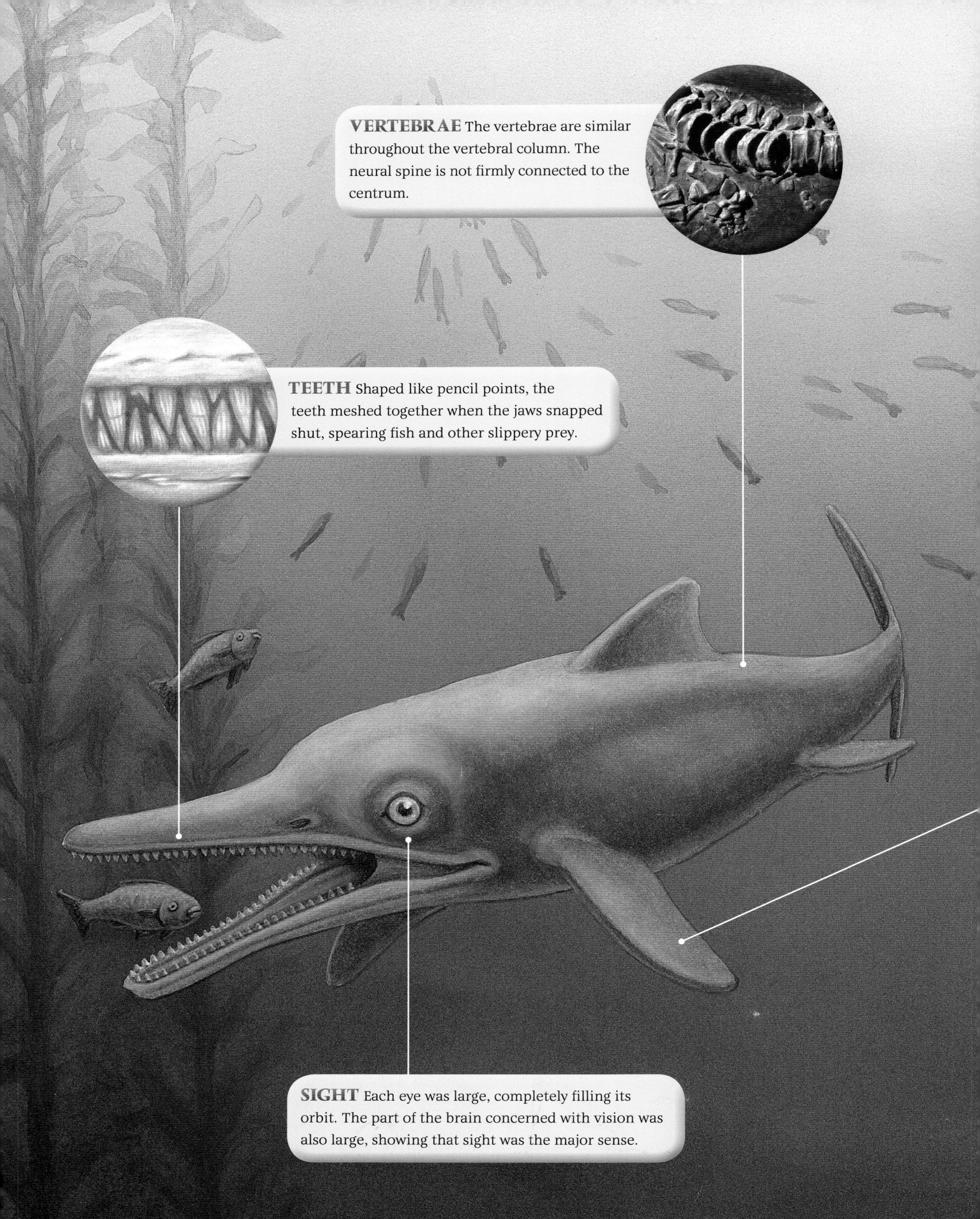

VERTEBRAE The vertebrae are similar throughout the vertebral column. The neural spine is not firmly connected to the centrum.

TEETH Shaped like pencil points, the teeth meshed together when the jaws snapped shut, spearing fish and other slippery prey.

SIGHT Each eye was large, completely filling its orbit. The part of the brain concerned with vision was also large, showing that sight was the major sense.

ICHTHYOSAURUS

(pronounced IK-thee-oh-SOR-us)

MEANING OF NAME:	"Fish reptile"
TYPE:	Ichthyosaur
AGE:	Late Triassic–Early Jurassic
LOCALITY:	Europe
LENGTH:	8 feet (2.5 m)

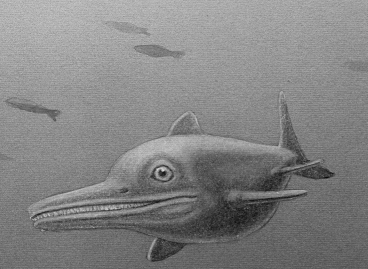

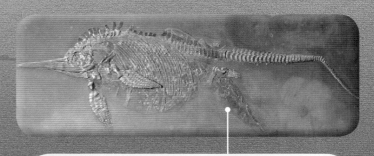

BIRTH Unlike most reptiles, which lay eggs, ichthyosaurs bore their young alive. Like whales, they were born tail first, to prevent drowning.

PAIRED FINS The bones of the fins are small and tightly packed together, so individual fingers are no longer obvious. The fins functioned like the diving planes of a submarine, to adjust the swimming level.

ICHTHYOSAURS ARE REPTILES THAT LIVED IN THE SEA while dinosaurs roamed the land. Thousands of skeletons have been found, sometimes remarkably complete, even with body outlines preserved as thin films. Streamlined like fish, they had paired fins instead of arms and legs, a sharklike **dorsal** fin on the back, and a tail for swimming. They ranged greatly in size—some were as small as salmon, others were as large as gray whales—but most were dolphin-size. *Ichthyosaurus* is a typical ichthyosaur, with its long bill crammed with teeth, large **orbits** (eye sockets), and simple vertebral column with a kink in the tail. It hunted fish and squidlike animals—their remains have been found inside its body. Baby ichthyosaurs have also been discovered there, but these were their offspring, not their food.

AIR TRIALS

Ichthyosaurs moved up and down by changing the tilt on their front fins. Imagine an animal swimming through the water. When the fins tilt upward, the water pushes against their undersides, lifting up the head end. If the fins tilt downward instead, the water pressure on the upper sides pushes the head down. You can check this out without getting wet.

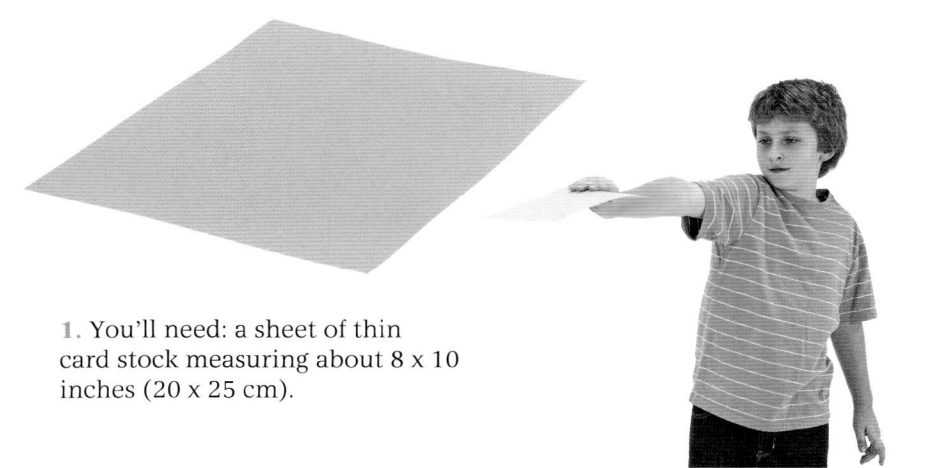

1. You'll need: a sheet of thin card stock measuring about 8 x 10 inches (20 x 25 cm).

2. Using your finger and thumb, hold the middle of a short edge in your right hand—the far end will droop down slightly. Stand up and straighten your arm to the side so that it's in line with your shoulder. Holding the card parallel with the floor, quickly sweep it forward by twisting your body to the left. Swish back and forward several times, still keeping it horizontal. Does anything happen to the card? Probably not—provided you kept it flat.

3. Now tilt the long left edge up a little, so that the card is angled to the floor. Quickly sweep the card forward, toward your left. This time the card lifts up—it's producing lift, like an airplane wing. When you swing back the other way, it gets pushed down.

STREAMLINES

If you look at a fish, like a salmon, you'll see it is widest in the front half of its body, tapering toward the head and tail. This streamlined body shape, seen in animals from whales to birds, helps them slip through water or air with least disturbance. You can make a streamlined body and see how it performs.

1. You'll need: modeling clay; a paper clip; thread; Scotch tape; a drinking straw; a bathtub one-third filled with cold water (as indicated here by the washtub); an aluminum pie plate; a pair of old scissors.

2. Roll the modeling clay into a ball 1 inch (2.5 cm) in diameter. Form this into a streamlined shape as shown.

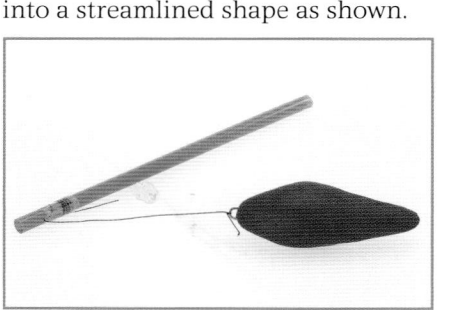

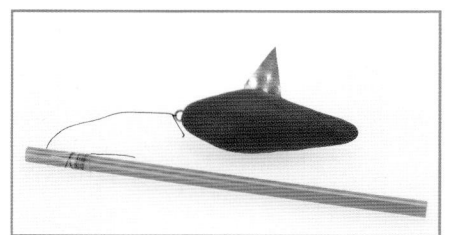

4. Now cut a triangular piece of aluminum 1 inch (2.5 cm) high and ¾ inch (2 cm) wide at its base. Keeping it in line with the body, press it into place as shown, with the front edge just behind the widest part of the streamline.

Break the narrow loop from the paper clip by prying it open and repeatedly bending it back and forth. Push the open end of this loop into the front of your streamline model. Tie one end of the thread to the loop. Tape the other end to one end of the straw, making the thread 3 inches (7.5 cm) long.

3. Tow the model through the water, keeping the straw just above the surface. Notice how the tail end wobbles. This is because there are no fins.

5. Tow the model through the water again. Do you notice less wobbling, and less vibration in the towing handle? Your fin adds stability.

You're now ready to build a pair of fins and try them out underwater.

1. You'll need: a pair of old scissors; a marker; an aluminum pie plate; some modeling clay; a pencil; a drinking straw; a washtub or sink almost full of water.

2. Mark and then cut out two aluminum fins, as shown in the photo. Make a modeling clay ball about ¾ inch (2 cm) in diameter. Flatten it into a doughnut, about ⅜ inch (1 cm) thick. Using a pencil, make a hole in the middle. Push the straw through the hole. Lay the straw and doughnut on the table, with the top of the straw pointing away from you. Use your finger and thumb to steady the doughnut. Using your other hand, hold one of the fins vertically, with the narrow side facing the table.

3. Keeping the fin vertical, press the narrow edge into the middle of the doughnut so that one corner is higher than the other. Adjust the modeling clay to hold the fin firmly in place. Stick the other fin into the other side, setting them both at the same angle.

4. Make a second modeling clay ball, like the first, and press it firmly onto one end of the straw—this will be the bottom. Check that the doughnut moves freely up and down.

5. Then, holding the top of the straw, lower your fins to the bottom of the washtub or sink, keeping close to one side. Line up your fins so that the upper edges face toward the other side of the washtub or sink. Keeping the straw vertical, sweep toward the far side. Your fins will rise in the water. If you quickly sweep the other way, before they sink, the water pressure will push them down.

IGUANODON

(pronounced ig-WAH-noh-DON)

MEANING OF NAME:	"Iguana tooth"
TYPE:	**Ornithopod**
AGE:	**Early Cretaceous**
LOCALITY:	**England, Europe, possibly North America**
LENGTH:	**33 feet (10 m)**

DINNER IN A DINOSAUR In 1854 Richard Owen, who coined the term "dinosaur," held a dinner party inside a replica of *Iguanodon*. This was shortly before completion of the life-size models of prehistoric animals for London's famous Crystal Palace.

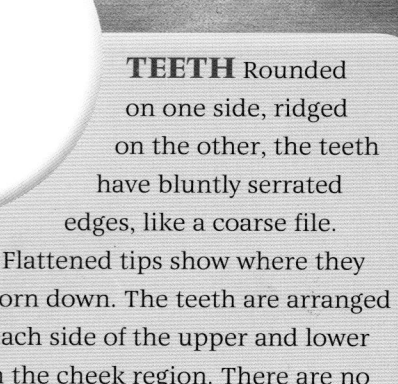

TEETH Rounded on one side, ridged on the other, the teeth have bluntly serrated edges, like a coarse file. Flattened tips show where they were worn down. The teeth are arranged along each side of the upper and lower jaws, in the cheek region. There are no front teeth.

GIDEON MANTELL, AN ENGLISH COUNTRY DOCTOR, LOVED PALEONTOLOGY. He regularly purchased fossils from local quarrymen and in 1821 obtained some unusual teeth. They were blunt, and as thick as his thumb, and he believed they belonged to a giant herbivorous reptile. Without realizing it, he'd discovered the world's first dinosaur. He named his find *Iguanodon* in 1825, but by then another dinosaur, *Megalosaurus*, had already been named. More than fifty years later and 1,000 feet underground, Belgian coal miners discovered dozens of *Iguanodon* skeletons—the first complete dinosaurs ever found.

Iguanodon probably walked on all fours, carrying most of its weight on the hind legs. The long tail balanced the weight of the rest of the body around the hips, like a teeter-totter. Toes and fingers were hoofed, but the thumb had a long spike, which may have been defensive. The cheek teeth chewed the plants cropped by the broad, horny beak.

BONY BRACES Much of the vertebral column is crisscrossed by pencil-thick bony rods, called **ossified tendons**. They helped stiffen the backbone.

Hundreds of hadrosaurs have been found, some with "mummified" skin, including complete skeletons; eggs; hatchlings; and juveniles, often in nests. These elephant-size herbivores roamed the land in great herds, cropping vegetation, the way buffalo once did. One remarkable feature is the number of cheek teeth—about one thousand—crammed into four grinding plates along the edges of the jaws. There are no other teeth. The front of the skull flares into a wide bill, like a duck's, which is why hadrosaurs are often called duck-billed dinosaurs. Many hadrosaurs have crests on their skulls, and *Parasaurolophus* has the most impressive. Inside is a long, U-shaped tube connecting the nostrils to the throat. This was probably used for trumpeting. You can hear how it may have sounded by visiting http://www.sandia.gov/media/dinosaur.htm. The sound is something like that of a trombone. Other hadrosaurs may have made sounds using their hollow crests too.

PARASAUROLOPHUS

(pronounced PAR-ah-saw-ROL-ah-fus)

MEANING OF NAME:	"Near crested reptile"
TYPE:	Hadrosaur
AGE:	Late Cretaceous
LOCALITY:	Western North America
LENGTH:	33 feet (10 m)

JAWS Both the upper and lower jaws are deep, to house the stacked columns of replacement teeth. The joint allowed the lower jaw to move back and forth and from side to side, as well as up and down.

— DID YOU KNOW? —

GOOD PARENTS The discovery of juveniles at the nest, along with hatchlings and adults, shows their parents were probably looking after them.

TEETH Hadrosaur teeth are like those of *Iguanodon*, but smaller and narrower. The hard enamel coating wore more slowly than the material inside, so this formed an outer ring—like a cone when you've licked away most of the ice cream. These sharp edges acted like the ridges of a file. As the teeth wore away, they were replaced by new ones from deeper down. The total number of teeth in a hadrosaur's mouth was more than a thousand. The upper and lower tooth rows ground against each other, pulverizing the plant food. Their ability to grind up food so effectively was probably one of the reasons why hadrosaurs were so successful.

HERBIVORE OR CARNIVORE?

Most clues to an animal's diet are found in the mouth. **Carnivores** have sharp teeth for killing and for slicing through flesh. **Herbivores** mostly have blunt teeth, for grinding plants. What do you think you are?

1. You'll need: a mirror; a big smile; chewing gum.

2. Look at your teeth in the mirror. You'll see they're all at about the same level. Slowly run your tongue along the tops of your teeth. Notice that your front teeth are narrow, and the back ones—your cheek teeth, which run along the sides of your mouth—are broad.

3. Chew some gum—two pieces should be enough. After rolling it into a ball with your fingers, flatten it into an oval pad to fit between your cheek teeth. Gently bite down, without cutting through. Check the tooth marks on either side of the gum. You'll find that the impressions are fairly wide. These teeth are for chewing rather than slicing. The dimples are made by the raised bumps on your teeth, called **cusps**—they help grind the food.

4. Repeat for your front teeth, as if biting into an apple. This time the tooth marks are narrow. Your front teeth, called **incisors**, are used for slicing.

Look at the photo of a cat skull on the left. Identify the **canine teeth** (they are the longest ones)—there are two pairs, upper and lower. Sharply pointed, they are used by carnivores to kill their prey. Can you see the incisors? They are the small teeth at the front, between the canines. Look at the large cheek teeth behind the canines. These teeth have cusps like blades and are used for slicing through flesh. A lion could chop through fingers with these teeth.

What are your canine teeth like? Look in the mirror. You have two incisors, top and bottom, on each side of your mouth. So the third tooth from the center is the canine. Is it sharp or blunt? Long or short?

Check out the photo of a horse skull on the right. The canine is the shortest tooth and is usually found only in males. The cheek teeth are broad and have ridged cusps, like a coarse file. The incisors are much broader than yours—they're used for chopping and pulling at plants.

Have you ever tried cutting thick cardboard using scissors with a loose joint? Instead of sliding past each other and cutting cleanly, the blades wobble from side to side and get jammed. To avoid a similar problem, the jaw joint of a carnivore has no sideways movement, so the jaw moves only up and down. Herbivores, in contrast, can waggle their jaws from side to side, which helps them grind up their food. Can you waggle your jaw?

Draw up a check list, marking your choices with ticks.

So what are you—a carnivore or an herbivore? You've probably found you're midway. Humans are neither carnivores nor herbivores. Like many other animals, such as raccoons, bears, and skunks, we are **omnivores**, eating a wide range of foods, including plants and animals.

We need to take care of our teeth because, like other **mammals**, once we get our grown-up secondary ones, that's it! Dinosaurs, like other reptiles, were luckier because their teeth were continually replaced. As their teeth wore down or got knocked out, they were replaced by new ones.

MUSICAL TUBES

Some specimens of *Parasaurolophus* have shorter crests than others. Would these have produced higher or lower notes? Find out with a simple experiment.

1. You'll need two drinking straws of different widths, so that one fits snugly inside the other.

2. Slip one straw inside the other. Hold them vertically, with the wider tube in one hand and the bottom of the narrow tube in the other. Push the narrow tube inside the other as far as it will go. Press your lower lip against the edge of the outer tube and blow, making a hissing, whistling noise.

3. While still blowing, lower the narrow tube. Does a longer tube make a higher or a lower note?

MAKING "MUMMIFIED" SKIN

"Mummified" hadrosaur skin is not really skin, but a sandstone replica made when a hadrosaur left an impression of its hide in the ground.

1. You'll need: 2 to 3 teaspoonfuls of clean, dry sand; a shallow container (like a paper plate or box lid); damp soil (enough to fill container); an unopened soda can; an ear of corn; clear nail polish; a knife; an old toothbrush. An adult helper could be useful. **Warning: Nail polish must be used in a well-ventilated room.**

2. Remove any lumps from the sand (you might need to sift it). Fill the container with the damp soil and roll it flat with the can. After removing the husk, firmly press the ear of corn into the soil, rocking it slightly from side to side to make a good impression.

3. After removing the corn, you will see the impression of several rows of kernels—an ear of corn has a pebbled surface something like a hadrosaur skin.

4. Carefully sprinkle sand into the impression, forming a thin layer.

5. Once it's covered, you can add the rest of the sand quickly, until it reaches the level of the soil. Drip nail polish onto the sand so that it soaks in, gluing the grains together. Leave it to dry for a day.

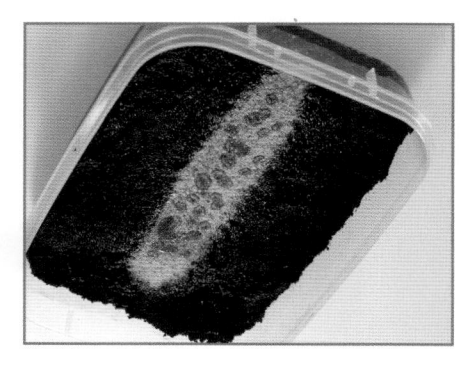

6. When your artificial sandstone feels hard, loosen the soil with a knife and lift it free.

7. Carefully scrape away the soil, stopping as soon as you reach the sand. (If your "sandstone" feels soft, let it harden for another day.) Brush off the last of the soil with the toothbrush. If this doesn't work, trickle cold water onto it, gently rubbing with your finger.

PLESIOSAURUS

(pronounced PLEES-ee-oh-SOR-us)

MEANING OF NAME: "Near reptile"
TYPE: Plesiosaur
AGE: Early Jurassic
LOCALITY: England, Germany
LENGTH: 10 feet (3 m)

NECK The neck has about forty vertebrae (we have seven) and was flexible. But it could not have bent like a swan's neck, as shown in some old illustrations.

MARY ANNING, one of the greatest fossil collectors, was twelve when she unearthed the first ichthyosaur and twenty-one or twenty-two when she discovered the first plesiosaur. She also found the first British pterosaur.

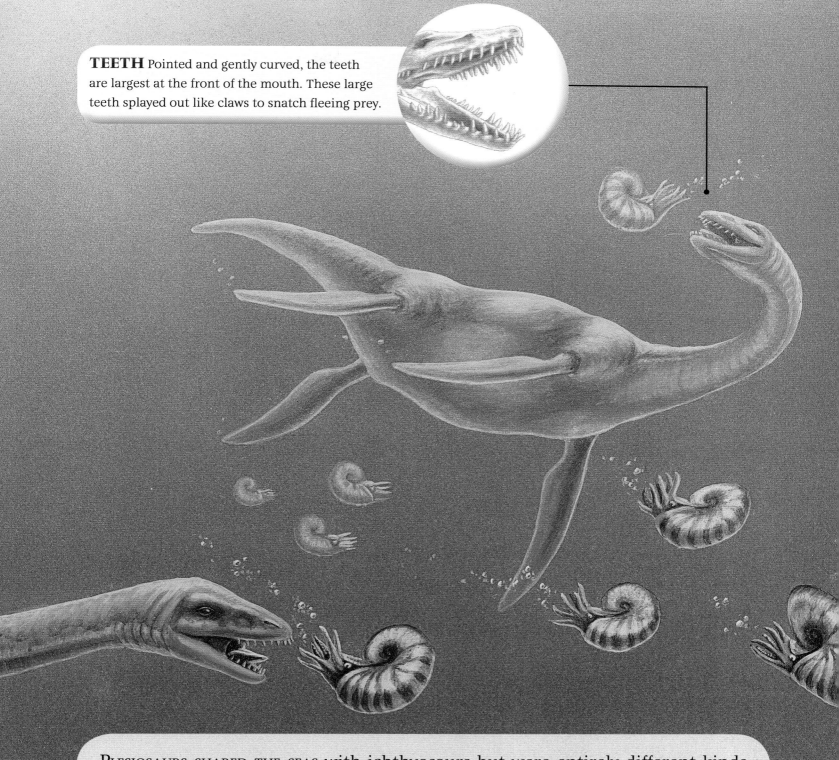

TEETH Pointed and gently curved, the teeth are largest at the front of the mouth. These large teeth splayed out like claws to snatch fleeing prey.

PLESIOSAURS SHARED THE SEAS with ichthyosaurs but were entirely different kinds of reptiles. There are two types—one group has small heads and long necks, the other has large heads and short necks. *Plesiosaurus*, the world's first, was discovered by Mary Anning in Lyme Regis, on England's Dorset coast, in 1820 or 1821 (the date is unclear because she didn't keep a record). Unlike *Ichthyosaurus* with its short fins, *Plesiosaurus* has long paddles, with five distinct fingers and toes. These paddles were used to propel it. The paddles would probably have been moved up and down like wings—the way penguins "fly" underwater. The shoulders and pelvis formed large plates in the chest and abdomen, to which the bulk of the muscles powering the flippers were attached.

UNDERWATER HEARING

Those flaps on the sides of your head—your ears—don't do very much. If they fell off, you'd still be able to hear. That's because the hearing part, called the **cochlea**, is inside your head.

When you hear a noise, you can tell where it's coming from because it's slightly louder in the ear closest to the sound. You can't tell directions underwater, though. That's because sound travels so easily through water and through your head that there's no difference in loudness between your two ears. But some animals, like whales, *can* tell directions underwater, and they use their ears for hunting by **echolocation**. They can do this because their inner ears are separated from each other by foam insulation so the sound is louder in the ear closest to their prey. Test your underwater hearing.

1. You'll need: an adult helper; a swimming pool; a pair of spoons.

2. Before getting into the pool, sit with your eyes shut and ask your helper to make a sound a few yards away. Without peeking, point toward the noise. Repeat several times. Are you satisfied you can locate sounds?

3. Stand up to your chin in the shallow end of the pool, with your eyes shut. Meanwhile, your helper should get into position beside the pool several yards away. Bend your legs so that your head is underwater. Have your helper bang the spoons together underwater. If you think you know the direction, turn around to face it. Now stand up and open your eyes. Were you right? Repeat several more times.

What about plesiosaurs? As with ichthyosaurs, the bones surrounding their two inner ears are in solid contact, as they are in your head, so they couldn't have located their prey by sound.

FLYING IN THE BATHTUB

How useful would the crest have been in steadying the head when *Pteranodon* was flying? Find out by making a model. As you don't have a **wind tunnel**, you can test it in the bathtub.

1. You'll need: a marker; an aluminum pie plate; a pair of old scissors; some modeling clay; a drinking straw; a half-filled bathtub (we've used a washtub here).

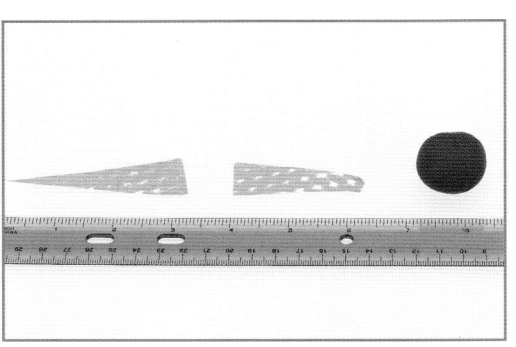

2. Using the plate, mark and then cut out two aluminum shapes as shown in the photo. The larger one is the bill, the other the crest. For the head, make a modeling clay ball about ¾ inch (2 cm) in diameter.

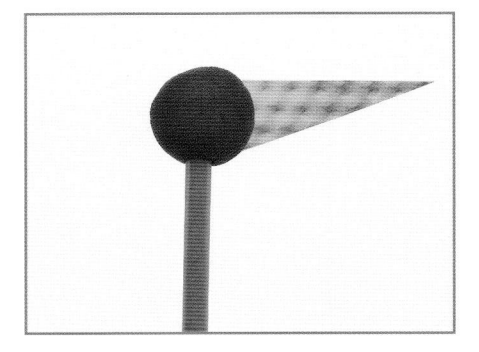

3. Attach the bill to the head by pressing the short edge into the middle of the ball. Pinch the modeling clay on either side to hold it firmly. As in the photo above, attach the straw perpendicular to the bill by twisting it as you push it into the bottom of the head. *Important*: Keep the straw in line with the bill. The crest is attached later.

4. Lower your model into the tub. Gently sweep it through the water, keeping the bill pointing forward. Is it hard to keep the head steady?

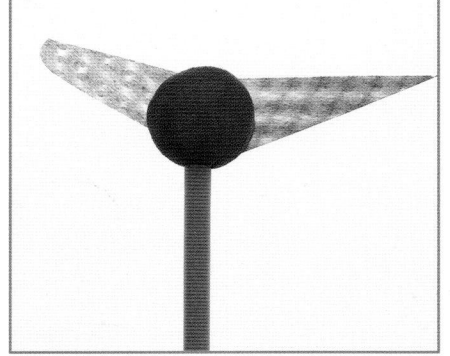

5. After several more sweeps, attach the crest as shown above. Sweep it through the water again. This time it's much easier to fly straight.

SWIM LIKE A PLESIOSAUR

Caution: This activity is only for competent swimmers and requires supervision of an adult.

1. You'll need: a swimming pool; an adult helper.

2. Float facedown on the surface with your arms outstretched to the sides. Press your fingers together and stretch out your hands, keeping them parallel to the surface. The front of your body is now a plesiosaur and these are your paddles. Don't worry about your legs—the back of your body is still human and will just tag along.

3. You're going to use your flippers like wings, but you have to keep tilting them for each beat. On the downstroke, your thumb has to be lower than your little finger. On the upstroke, your thumb has to be higher. Give it a try. To help get the hang of it, you could practice the stroke sitting beside the pool.

You won't beat any Olympic records! And you might think you're standing still, but if you check the edge of the pool, you'll see you're moving. Like a plesiosaur, your downstroke is more powerful than your upstroke. That's because the muscles pulling your paddles down are bigger than those pulling them up.

BONE SANDWICH

The crest of *Pteranodon* is only about ⅛ inch (3 mm) thick, getting its strength from the way it is built. It's simply two thin sheets joined together by spongy bone—as light as cotton candy. You can fake some yourself.

1. You'll need: cardboard (you can use a cereal box); scissors; waxed paper; glue (Crayola Project Glue or UHU Twist & Glue); a drinking straw; Rice Krispies; a small pile of books.

2. Cut out four strips of cardboard, each 1 x 5 inches (2.5 x 13 cm). Place one strip on a piece of waxed paper and spread evenly with a *thin* layer of glue, using the straw. Sprinkle with Rice Krispies, covering the entire surface. You need a *single* layer, so shake off the extras.

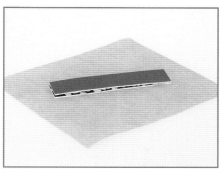

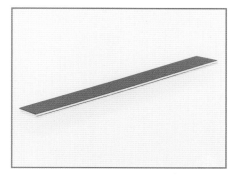

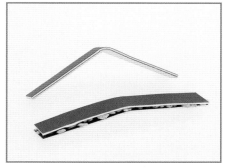

3. Thinly coat a second strip and place it, glue side down, on top of the Rice Krispies. Press down *gently* but firmly. Cover with waxed paper and place two or three books on top—not big ones, and the pile shouldn't be more than 3 inches high.

4. Glue the other two strips together, pressing them between waxed paper under several books. Leave both sets of strips for 2 hours. Uncover and leave them to dry for 6 hours.

5. How do the two strips compare? Gently bend the thin one. Notice how easily it flexes. Repeat for the Rice Krispies sandwich. Are you surprised at how much stiffer it is? To make an even stronger—and neater—sandwich, repeat the experiment, substituting five drinking straws—cut to 5-inch (13 cm) lengths—for the Rice Krispies and using lots of glue.

PTERANODON

(pronounced ter-RAN-oh-DON)

MEANING OF NAME: "Winged and toothless"
TYPE: Pterosaur
AGE: Late Cretaceous
LOCALITY: Western North America
LENGTH: 26 feet (8 m) wingspan

CREST The thin crest occupies almost half of the 6-foot-long (2 m) skull. Its main function may have been to act as a rudder, steadying the head during flight.

FEEDING *Pteranodon* lived by the sea, and fish have been found in their stomachs. In one specimen, some fish remains lay below the jaws, showing there was probably a throat pouch like a pelican's.

WINGS The skin of the wings was probably elastic—more like a balloon than plastic wrap. Microscopic struts running across the wings' width helped to strengthen them.

FLYING *Pteranodon* was too big to flap its wings, except on takeoff and landing. Once airborne, it would soar on the wind, like today's albatross.

WALKING Experts disagree on whether *Pteranodon* was bipedal or quadrupedal. Walking on all fours seems more likely. It was probably not a good walker.

APPEARING 80 MILLION YEARS BEFORE *ARCHAEOPTERYX*, pterosaurs were the first vertebrates to fly by flapping. The earliest ones had long, bony tails, but these kinds became extinct and all the later ones had short tails. Pterosaurs have only four fingers. The first three—equivalent to our thumb, index finger, and middle finger—are short, but the fourth is enormously long and supported the wings, which were made of the thinnest skin. Pterosaurs range from the size of sparrows to the size of small aircraft, and *Pteranodon* is one of the largest. Its hollow bones are even more lightly built than those of birds—barely thicker than cardboard. The toothless skull has a long, narrow bill, like a pelican's, with a huge crest at the back. The back legs splayed out at the sides and were probably attached to the wings at the thighs.

BODY COVERING The longest strands are about 1½ inches (40 mm) long. The thickest strands are much coarser than the hair of most small mammals.

TEETH The front teeth are fairly straight and smooth. The back ones are broad and curved like daggers, with serrations on the inside edge.

HANDS Although the hands are not large, they are almost as long as the arms. All three fingers end in sharp claws.

SINOSAUROPTERYX

(pronounced SINE-oh-sore-OP-ter-ix)

MEANING OF NAME: "Chinese feathered reptile"
TYPE: Theropod
AGE: Late Jurassic or Early Cretaceous
LOCALITY: Liaoning Province, China
LENGTH: 4 feet (1.2 m)

THIS SMALL DINOSAUR IS UNUSUAL FOR ITS EXTREMELY LONG TAIL, which is twice the length of the rest of its body. The arms are remarkably short and powerfully built and were probably used for attacking prey. What makes *Sinosauropteryx* so special, though, is that it was the first dinosaur discovered with evidence of feathers. These are not the familiar feathers of birds, but wispy strands, like hair, that covered the body. Keeping the animal warm seems their most likely function, which shows that *Sinosauropteryx* was warm-blooded. Since its discovery in 1996, several more dinosaurs have been found with feathery coverings, ranging from strands to typical feathers. These discoveries support the idea that birds and dinosaurs are closely related. Indeed, birds are classified as theropods, and paleontologists refer to all other theropods, like *Tyrannosaurus* and *Sinosauropteryx*, as nonavian (nonbird) theropods.

THE WIDER THE BETTER

Some pterosaur bones, like the humerus, are surprisingly broad. This is because wide tubes are much stronger and stiffer than narrow ones. You can test this yourself.

1. You'll need: a piece of paper; scissors; the screw cap from a juice carton (or milk jug); Scotch tape; a twist tie; two unopened soda cans; two drinking straws—one regular, one wide (like you get with milk shakes); a marker; a handful of identical coins—not larger than quarters.

2. Cut out a 3 x 8 inch (7 x 20 cm) paper strip. Note: If you're using a bigger cap than from a juice carton, make the strip 2 inches (5 cm) wide. Lay the cap upside down on a table and wrap the paper strip around it. Tape the end down, then run another strip of tape beneath the cap. You've now got a container to hold the coins. Complete this by attaching the twist tie as a carrying handle.

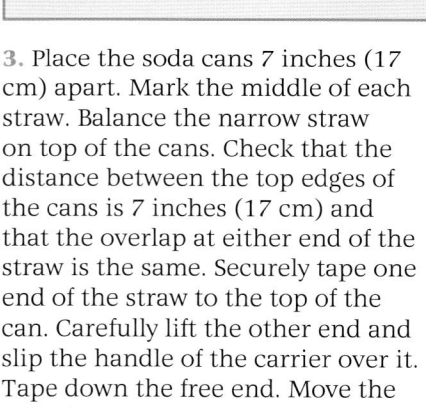

3. Place the soda cans 7 inches (17 cm) apart. Mark the middle of each straw. Balance the narrow straw on top of the cans. Check that the distance between the top edges of the cans is 7 inches (17 cm) and that the overlap at either end of the straw is the same. Securely tape one end of the straw to the top of the can. Carefully lift the other end and slip the handle of the carrier over it. Tape down the free end. Move the container so that the handle is in the middle of the straw.

4. Add coins, one at a time, steadying the container each time. Keep count. Continue until the sagging straw gives way and bends. Note how many coins it took.

5. Repeat the experiment with the wider straw. Are you surprised at how much stronger it is?

EYES FRONT

Our eyes, like those of cats and hawks, face forward. The overlap between left and right eyes is what gives us **binocular vision**, allowing us to see things in 3-D. Check how well you can do things with, and without, binocular vision.

1. You'll need: a marker; a pencil.

2. Mark a dot on the end of one of your fingers. Hold a pencil by the blunt end in the other hand and stretch out your arm. Try touching the dot with the pencil tip. Spread your arms wide apart and repeat. Do this ten times, changing the position of your finger each time. How many times did you succeed? Repeat this experiment with one eye closed. What's your score now? Are you convinced you need binocular vision to judge distances?

FLUFFY POTATOES

Feathers make good insulation. You can check this for yourself by making some artificial ones from paper.

1. You'll need: paper towels; a cup; an adult helper; two potatoes about 2 inches (5 cm) in diameter—they must be the same size; a microwave (or saucepan and stove); gloves; a pencil and notepad; a knife.

2. Using your finger and thumb, tear off small pieces of paper towel about 1 inch (2.5 cm) long and drop them in the cup. You need at least three cupfuls. Ask your adult helper to cook the potatoes in a microwave at full power for 1½ to 2 minutes, until they sizzle (or bring them to a boil in a saucepan). Meanwhile, heap a cupful of "feathers" into a small pile. Wearing gloves, quickly dry both potatoes with paper towels.

3. Place one potato onto the pile of "feathers," heaping the rest on top. Put the other potato beside it.

4. Take a note of the time. After 18 minutes, pick up the uncovered potato. How hot is it? Write this down. Keep checking every 2 minutes, writing down the results. When the uncovered potato feels warm, check the insulated one, quickly covering it up afterward. Did it feel hot? Make a note. When the uncovered potato feels barely warm, check the other one. Make another note. Cut each potato in half, placing the cut end on the back of your hand. Which one is warmer?

CASTING TEETH

You are *Tyrannosaurus*, about to sink your teeth into *Triceratops*. Sixty-five million years later a paleontologist makes a **cast** (replica) of your teeth from the impressions you left in the bone.

1. You'll need: modeling clay; plaster of paris; water; a teaspoon; a small container.

2. Roll a piece of modeling clay into a ball 1½ inches (3.8 cm) in diameter. Gently press it down onto a table, flattening the bottom a little, so that the ball will stay in place.

3. Hold the top of the ball against your top teeth and press up steadily until your teeth have sunk in all the way to the gum line. Carefully remove by gently pulling down with both hands, making sure to pull in line with your teeth. Place the ball on the table.

4. Notice that your tooth impressions (the **mold**) slope down the sides of the ball. To prevent the plaster from dribbling out, you need to add thin sheets of modeling clay at either end, smoothing them onto the ball.

5. Add 1 teaspoon of plaster and the same amount of water to your container, mixing well. Your plaster should be runny, like cream. Work fast because the plaster thickens quickly. Pour it into your mold. When it's full, gently tap your mold on the table for 30 seconds to release the air bubbles to the surface. Leave it to set for *at least* 2 hours. Carefully break the modeling clay away from the cast of your teeth.

TYRANNOSAURUS
(pronounced tie-RAN-oh-SOR-us)

MEANING OF NAME:	"Terrible reptile"
TYPE:	Theropod
AGE:	Late Cretaceous
LOCALITY:	Western North America
LENGTH:	46 feet (14 m)

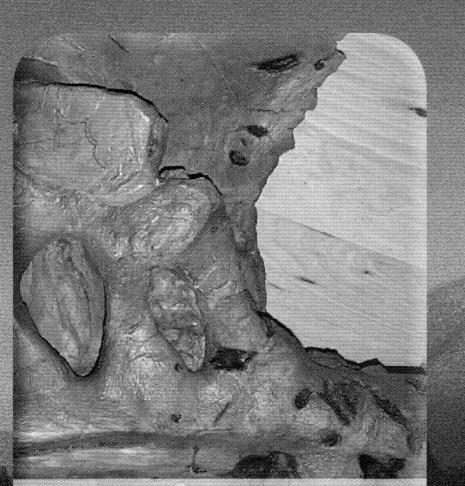

Tooth marks in a *Triceratops* bone

SIGHT With eyes as big as oranges, *Tyrannosaurus* may have had sharper vision than our own, possibly allowing it to see objects several miles away. The eyes faced forward rather than to the sides, giving *Tyrannosaurus* binocular vision. This is vital for predators, as it enables them to judge distances so that they can catch their prey.

WEIGHING MORE THAN AN AFRICAN ELEPHANT, *Tyrannosaurus* was probably the largest predator to stalk the earth. Some paleontologists believe its jaws and teeth were too weak to tackle a struggling dinosaur, and that it was a scavenger instead. However, there are clues to the enormous strength of its bite. First, large tooth marks have been found in a *Triceratops* skeleton. When replicas of the teeth were made by pouring liquid rubber into the holes, the casts were identical to the teeth of *Tyrannosaurus*. Another unexpected discovery was some dinosaur dung that contained shattered dinosaur bone. Given its huge size, the dung *had* to belong to *Tyrannosaurus* because that was the only large predator at that particular fossil locality.

Replica of *Tyrannosaurus* tooth

SKULL The back of the skull is wider than in *Allosaurus*, so the orbits faced partly forward, giving *Tyrannosaurus* some binocular vision.

SMELL X-ray scans of the braincase show that the part of the brain used for smelling was especially large—*Tyrannosaurus* had a good sense of smell.

TEETH Most of the 10-inch-long (25 cm) tooth was buried in the jaw, making it difficult to tear from the socket.

BLOOD While looking at some well-preserved *Tyrannosaurus* bone tissue under a microscope, paleontologists were startled to find blood cells, and even some blood vessels that were still elastic!

apatite: the calcium mineral in bone.

articular: relating to a joint. Articular surfaces of bones are capped with cartilage.

binocular vision: sight that uses two forward-pointing eyes. Binocular vision allows animals to judge distances.

bipedal ("two-footed"): walking on two legs. Humans, birds, and many dinosaurs are bipedal.

canine tooth: an especially long and sharp tooth in carnivores that is used for killing prey.

carnivore: a meat-eating animal. Lions and wolves are carnivores.

cast: a replica of an object, made by pouring a liquid substance into a mold, then letting it set.

center of mass (center of gravity): the balance point of an object.

cochlea: the hearing part of the ear. The term comes from the Greek word for "snail" because of the coiled shape.

collagen: the protein in bone that makes it slightly springy.

cusp: a raised point on the biting surface of a tooth.

dorsal: situated on the back as opposed to the front. Your shoulders are dorsal to your ribs.

echolocate: to use high-pitched sounds that bounce back from an object to determine where it is. Whales and bats echolocate to navigate and to find food.

femur: the thighbone.

herbivore: a plant-eating animal. Horses are herbivores.

incisors: the front teeth, usually chisel shaped.

ligament: the tough material, often like string, that joins bones together.

mammal: a warm-blooded animal that has hair or fur, and that feeds its young with milk. Mammals range from mice to horses to humans.

mold: the impression of an object, like a tooth impression in modeling clay.

mount: to assemble a skeleton.

nuchal ligament: a ligament at the back of the neck that connects to the skull. Humans and most other mammals have them. Unlike most ligaments, it is extremely elastic.

omnivore: an animal that eats both meat and plants. Humans are omnivores.

orbit: the eye socket.

ossified tendons: the bony rods that strengthened the vertebral column of some dinosaurs.

quadrupedal ("four-footed"): walking on four legs. Most mammals are quadrupedal.

Saurischia ("lizard-hipped"): a large grouping of dinosaurs comprising theropods and sauropods. All the others belong to the Ornithischia ("bird-hipped").

sauropod ("reptile-foot"): a group of large quadrupedal dinosaurs that includes *Apatosaurus*.

sedimentary rock: layered rocks formed by the settling of particles, usually in water.

theropod ("beast-foot"): a large group of animals that includes carnivorous dinosaurs like *Tyrannosaurus* and also birds.

ventral: situated on the bottom or front—the opposite of dorsal. Your navel is ventral to your hips.

vertebrate: an animal with a backbone. Vertebrates range from fishes and frogs to ducks and dolphins.

wind tunnel: a passageway equipped with a fan, often used for testing aircraft models.

zygapophyses (singular: **zygapophysis**): paired joint surfaces at the front and back of a vertebra.

Note: Page references in **boldface** refer to main descriptions of each dinosaur.